STET

PRINCETON SERIES OF CONTEMPORARY POETS
Susan Stewart, series editor

For other titles in the Princeton Series of Contemporary Poets see page 69

STET

Poems

Dora Malech

PRINCETON UNIVERSITY PRESS
Princeton and Oxford

Published by Princeton University Press
41 William Street, Princeton, New Jersey 08540
6 Oxford Street, Woodstock, Oxfordshire OX20 1TR

press.princeton.edu

Library of Congress Control Number: 2018931015

ISBN: 978-0-691-18143-1

ISBN (pbk.) 978-0-691-18144-8

British Library Cataloging-in-Publication Data is available

Acquisitions Editor: Anne Savarese
Editorial Assistant: Thalia Leaf
Production Editorial: Ellen Foos
Text and Cover Design: Pamela Schnitter
Cover art: *Polyphonie* (2011) by Fabienne Verdier
Production: Jacqueline Poirier
Copyeditor: Daniel Simon

This book has been composed in Adobe Garamond Pro and ScalaSansOT

Printed on acid-free paper. ∞

Printed in the United States of America

10 9 8 7 6 5 4 3 2 1

FOR [   ]

Acknowledgments

The author wishes to thank the Amy Clampitt Fund for a 2017 Amy Clampitt Residency Award, the Poetry Foundation for a 2010 Ruth Lilly Poetry Fellowship, the Civitella Ranieri Foundation for a 2009 Writing Residency Fellowship, and the editors of the following publications in which some of these poems first appeared:

> *Bennington Review* ("As[   ]k," "[   ]or[   ]ask[   ]"); *Hidden City Quarterly* ("sure   ruse," "[Cos(ign]eous)," "a time balm"); *Horsethief* ("After Plath: Metaphors" III, VI, VIII, IX); *jubliat* ("The *can't not*'s   the constant"); *PEN America* ("Assail   as sail   ails as," "Descreation Myth," "Stet"); *Sidereal* ("Road Not End," "[See: erosion]," "Something wonderful is about to happen to you," "then reading   in the garden"); *Sprung Formal* ("Cry unto   Country"); *Tin House* ("Are not   no tear"); *Unsplendid* ("Q & A," "This, Certain"); *Versal* ("Daisies   is ideas").

The author also thanks Michelle Falkoff, Joseph Harrison, Kristin Kelly, and Kyle Stine for believing in these poems and thanks Jane Lewty for her support and insights throughout the years this book took its form(s).

Contents

Scrawling the letters of my name,
I found and changed what I became:

—Henri Cole, "Anagram"

STET

ESSAY   AS YES,

begged off bad beginnings, false starts of a star-sat self, her benched head cartoon bird spun, stunned out a long season. I came to claim I wouldn't burden you with the trailed-off scrap heap of all the times I tried to explain (plain) already, but even without evidence of wadded paper, snowdrift of not that, it is those attempts that act as apologia, sense in absence, itinerant iterations' cairns at the crossroads, hobo code in chalk or coal, worlds not long for these words. In other words: in other words, diary's everyday no entry, inverse relationship between clarity and efficacy. I needed forms that could flail, fail, lists listing back toward their not-so-fresh catalysts, sepsis of afterbirth still lodged in the body, that which once nurtured lingering malignant.

The I, just talk: just like that. Same went for the you(s): free on what messy out. I didn't want to spill it—it meaning guts, etcetera, but mostly guts—because they weren't all mine to spill, those two tin cans strung from the ends of viscera, the what-we-listen-to and where-we-feel-it, so to speak. In my belly, twisted sum [sic] sine in test. It's an old story, sure, and came in waves. I left my name at the front desk. I waved. I left. Abbreviation: sin. The take lodged in to speak that leaves us P.S., postscript as remaindered O, sighed apostrophe to what we turn away (from).

Even some years later, when the nurse explained the blood test, I felt the familiar flush as something else made sense. Material released: information that circulates in the bloodstream. To point to the center and say there wasn't quite right after all. There were bits of the story flowing through me. In fact, the old imperative, echo of act in the sense of what's done. Is done. What is, in a manner of speaking, riveted to the text? In his anagram notebooks, Saussure said God(s) and named names.

Of this, the scholar writes, "Language's tokens make sense because they cor-respond." Raise your hand if you're who here can't hear the heart.

Under wraps, rapture, sous rature's insistent autocorrect. The trace createth (archaic ache) Zürn's "old, dangerous fever," Mackey's "exegetic sweat": open (source, sesame, letter, book). Pen, stain one mouth [and] the mountain opens. Bromine cant: recombinant. The lab in labial, the utter in, well, utter. Late tale: I hold the same old doll as me. Not a simulacrum left that the bad birds haven't pecked up, antipathetic, now violet night, violent insight. Cite anti-path as no road home, lips lit [to] spill it.

It turns out, it doesn't matter what we want to want because the spell still (ill saint) outs us, solves for scar in viscera where viscera is crave, cavity-crammed. Still an I, I was trying to write a beginning and an ending at once, using the only words my tongue could touch. Muddle and middle. The writing on the wall was a tunnel under cell-scratched time. Say law [of] always: simultaneous is nauseous limits. They weren't all mine to spill, and even their spooled length unfurled and measured didn't feel like all at all. Totality of utterance reduced to trance, to tatter.

Note burden's sense, too, as refrain, as what we carry singing down the road. Love me little, love me long's the bindle shouldered by that us that must end anonymous, bound to the stone of a song. With, across, after: referred myself to a different doctor, wielded the old ax in ask, metathetic. Closed eyes and metalept: hung for a moment in the air from where the bridge I burned once was. The best I could do was an embarrassment, crying for do-over, blushes reread, reacts in redactions. Or is it that the space was always there, and necessary, not absence but aperture, artery's foramen, foreman speaking for the jury?

Waved, left: laved weft, crosswise threads of a cloth washed and wrung, hung to dry on an over-under. An old story, spun whole cloth: blue banner shook upstage to make the sea's surge billow back the act. The sine was swell and sag. The sine was pregnant, pause, pregnant, pause.

Called hum [sic], hone [sic], a song sharpened in the singing, then ground to gone. Sic transit authority (see [sic] changes in signage): mind the [God of the] gap[s]. I always forgot the second I in liaison, and the screen scratched its red line ragged below our best in trysts [sic] (something in us) as I tried to make a dance of distance, move on. Something thumb sings of tapping into: the smallest screen's green flame, time-stamped out but still smoldering, or, hinge-stung, the rise in bruise as blood's chorus roars out its resistance. It's not exactly the same seam, but remove or rearrange and the trace remains, asks after, echoes back into and of its origins—

THE *CAN'T NOT'S* THE CONSTANT

If *now*, then   *when*, not *if.*

If *so*, this rented vow   redshifts.
                         View onto

baby's *bye-*   *bye*, baby's

*no give it*s. Spectrum shows all   this.
                              Love's trip came slow-sung

as in an era before me,   *be for me.* Erase an *a* in

erase to *ere's* is to   stare, sore *I see.* To

a note undid,   in and outed,

tides   sited,

a way waves   away, waves

            and did I?   I did. *And*

            do I?   I do.

Is as sight   sits a sigh,

what one calls *priors*   chase *now, ors.* I'll trap

as finger,   ring-safe,

forever, I said.   Or I said *fever.*

No matter in either.

            I   am not in the rite.
                                        I re-

spoke free.

        Ask,   for keep's sake.

4

AS[   ]K

Or else I said *ash*,   as I do.

                                      Selah, rise

to it, all *not*   *lit* at.

                              No lot

empty or otherwise
swore the pity more
empty or otherwise
poor.

               Yes, threw time
hope,

               swore *try it* (me).
Empty or otherwise

they wire:

                         MORE STOP

lie all evocative,   i.e., I'll vacate love.

A timid   *I admit*

I want out   *now*, taut, I

added *need*,   dead ended

en route.

                   Seems I'm sewn too tight.

                                        Spit me
to shine.

               Moot emesis.

                         Wept *rust me.*

                                   Get in.

Sometimes we step into something true.

Woke in the wake of   he knew too.

                              Weak *if,*

*then*s.

          Us,   the sun's

to set null, red into its   unset still, rode into T-

minus us,   us, in sum,

can't solve.

              Love's cant:

forever.

              Veer for

flingable alibi set:

                         all in a big life.

                              Best

caress   scares

revile   relive

a page   agape,

snag   nags

blink to   ink blot

gives a   visage,

eyes I'd made.   Seed my idea

in deed,   indeed,

fit end to law:

              pray   and we flap.

                         I try to

fly as time.

              Time flays

and falls on us,   and falls on us

to (hint:

          I dove   into the void)

6

destroy   (de-story).

I to pen:

> *open it.*

Re:

    man down,   remand now.

Re:

    mind over, I'd   err on mid-dive,

tender   rented

enemy   (née *my*)

in me,   mine

and in you, mine.

            I'm an end in you,

shrill *gone,*   her song.

                I'll

tithe   the it

'til   lit

into.

    Now,   in two.

            No

daisy stems clone   in a closed system,

cloud as I was there, the *no sweat,* led a
swan to water, sea, the leashed I could,
nice as dust, a low *oh, sweetheart, <u>deal</u>.*

This reader leafs   dearer, faithless.

A stress   rests as

I take words back, as   I so backward stake

blunt end.
                    Do,   *don't.*
                              Un-bled,

sit up to on-again,
out a song, I pan it
to no gain as I put

it out of.
                    Out of it,

our west ghost   wrought, so set

is as ore, haze on   a horizon, eases

at the speeds of dark,   asks the ode-fed part

who dies satisfied,   who is fisted aside,

as a *not her*,   as another

one's raw kiss, this
rain so skews, hits
skin, washes.
                    I sort

votes, events, abated oars, or
nod to stars (see above) avert
a verse.
          End starts above too,
starts to see over and above,
sines *I*.

          Batter knows ash,
hits awaken bones, stirs

and sees to start over.
          Above,

no ink bares with stases,
no rash bets.
          I sweat, sink
ask in a torn *best wishes*.
Rise, sawn shaken to bits,
beset as rain knows this
wit, the broken assassin,
no strike.
          Beasts wash in
on sins, hawks, batteries,
bats, twine, sharks, noise,
wet trash, ibis, snakes, no-
show ark's bent assent:
                    I—I—

wish best on an asterisk.

[   ]OR[   ]ASK[   ]

man   damned   forsakes
form and needs a mask

and form masks a need
and makes amends for

STET

Last meme down: to off our inner faith in
lit ions, amen (*fin*), fume of tore and throw,
stone hid unfelt, from "we" (from an "I" to an "I").
Nil with rot, a minute off deforms an eon
of meat run low, no foment, a tired finish,
mere sunlit affair. Oh, to find moon, went
wet at dim. Afternoon sinner, hum if fool
is true of mow, of annihilated front-men,
stunt-man, of him, an indoor Eiffel Tower,
non-sonata writ mute. For me, no HD life. If
radio, some worn tune. Then, main lift-off:
off-line, not no raft, I swim out here. Damn
if'n I wasted no moment of hurt on a rifle.
Old "No room at the inn," i.e., FU. Warn: stiff me
One time, shame on, off, until worn adrift.
Must we fail in one form to find another?

Cogs & cogs that cannot turn
*   to recognitions: such dogs in the dark noonday!*

As if the tongue told & tolled
Among
*   the melancholic arcades.*

Where the moods *advance toward the* modes.

Time to try the knot, the Not
Or to be caught
Forever in nerve-traceries of Beauty . . .

Unstrung, the structure is sound.

—Andrew Joron, "Mazed Interior"

FACE TO HEX

the letters

given   re-awaken

little   birth   of   language
                              sent   to
          decompose ,   re-compose
    .
      inspect   the   violent
                          form   , the
                          cause of
knowledge -   -   the   "other"
                    sense of
                the given letters   called

          toward   fever
                                    to play   or
          out
                          this   necessary   possible.
      one   would leave
              one's self
      at stake   , meaning   :   into
                          written   sudden   into
  sound.
mirrors
      hand   over   the wonder of   a
room
      ,
                    praise
                    as   ink   , as   error

          .

LAY AND   TRY

touching   the origins of

the   line

is   to

question

form

and

function

proceed   in the   mind,

create for it   a   different

"   life",   tie

logic and

magic

to   an   ear

.

DAISIES   IS IDEAS

O anther,   another   (no heart-

                                        twine)—

I went   in wet

                from   form

to find the vein—   vine fed to thin

off all bets,   best of fall

in amber enamored—
an aim (end) re-rob me
(near bromide amen)—
no bride ran a meme
nor bade me remain—

    *

All bets off,   fall best of

his stammering sin: hammers sing *isn't I*   *–isms* (sight 'n
    remain),   shimmering stains,

strike through,   rough the skirt—

    *

open carry,   a prone cry—

pray tend to you, rote:
        and you're too pretty . . .
        and you're pretty too . . .

sibilant shibboleth,   babble *sin this*, oh, lit,
I hint: *both-able bliss*

to thought—I, a game and   ought to (had I a magnet).

*

Felt   left—

daisies   dies as I

mean   (name)—

*

Now shot, I cut what swath?

This won't wash (*watch*) out—

ASSAIL   AS SAIL   AILS AS

I task—   *ask it.*
As sign   sings a

        post-   *STOP,*
          bleeds past,   pleads best

our nil fetters   in four letters,
claims curse,   claims cures,

tries   rites,

        tires—

          I rest

so after hope's test,   step so to the fears
in a red address,   redress, and aid,

after my fashions,   say offer's in math,
in simple subtraction,   in traction, sub *simple*

for, *like*, minds,   skid line from
my *you're all mine*s,   null. Yes, more *may I*?

        Alas, no.   Also an

obit—an . . . *and better   torn at, bite, and be,*
than never . . . and so on.   None. On. Hand averts

real day, an end rote. Intuit or thank your god
or do one in. And take your tight turn, already.

DESCREATION MYTH

Lay a waste from out thy ode.

            What to do after you slay me?

Start anew, lifeless.

         Start a new life, less

servant to order than

         très avant throne. Rod,

sweet slaughter.

      Sweet's laughter

supersedes repose,

        seeds so pure. Spree:

stun me. Stain us. O lab

           most unsustainable,

slab on which slit to mend means

            moan me silent, switch, lash, bond,

warmed-over meals of pieces stolen,

           slow violence of parts. See me armed.

Sweet meter, I'm a soft sum. Hone thy mark. Mark

            why monsters must make meat of their maker.

SURE   RUSE

neither *well*   *well i nether*   nor Babel-   able born:

 a veil   alive   in camera's   manic eras:

shot math well   hot math's *well*   *that'll show 'em*

numbers underfoot   our dumb front seen-

through gauntlet   late-rung thought

no   double   positive   (i've   no   doubt   I   slope)
no   double   positive   (i've   bled   out   poison)
no   double   positive   (stoop: be   unloved: *i   i*

                    yes yes   yes yes)

agitates machine wishable   aching is the blame (wait: sea)

                    ruined   inured

tine to a best touch   cut those into a bet

                    ink bling   blinking

automated and here we are   out where a dead ear meant

                in re: verse   sever in re-

turn is let through the   turnstile (the through

                    it and thrown)   hand not writ

                raw sending out   sounding water

as inking   a sinking   spit   pits   animates   as *name it*

outbid: i   do   (but   i   doubt)

our   islanded   odds   the   eden   blown
(this   need   doubles   older   and   down)

ARE NOT   NO TEAR

from   form
for to rest upon,   rent of, stop our
notes'   onset.
O sentence   once tense,
skin   inks
indelible, was   libel, sawed in
a shelf   aflesh.
In meat,   I meant,   in meat
begin   being
read,   dear,   a red
season   as one's
affairs   afar, ifs
in wet blossom   blown, so I stem.
Flower   flew, or
eros   rose,
or trees   reset, or
please   elapse
is lips,   is lips.   *I* slips
it into night.   In tonight, it
plays   splay,
sore throats' dins I   shored into stars. I
read   *dare*
to be a snow-pure   re-up, a bet won so
on aim,   on *I am*,
throw   worth
its harm,   this arm,
mute song   sung to me,
a moot   *am too.*

[SEE: EROSION]

the wave	arrives:
hewer	rives:
heave	aves:
hear	*is:*

To be at odds with

                              my-

self resounded, sound's own City the wall I hit

    my head against, polis was to be and to be so hit . . .

We heard clamor, clash, blue consonance, noise's

                                  low

    sibling

sense

—Nathaniel Mackey, "As If It Were 'This Is Our Music'"

A TIME BALM

at blame i'm

best and   stab end

up.   up

tick: is   it sick?

i split   its lip.

in your bad   body, a ruin.

step in it.   i spent it,

a zilch-and-die   child in a daze.

i snatched up   thus, paced in

auto-enclaves   a love can't use.

shut thus,   thus, shut.

rise shut. canticle,   this cut is cleaner.

WRIT IN ORE

Assume as muse,
muses:
            us, a seam.

TEST

it's not that it doesn't work, it's that it can't hold a charge.
replace   meant   so   sighted,   pester   this   day,
this   I   sent   to   best   there,   aims   overt,
wet   the   least   stone   too   late
ever   only   after   its   scare   struck   the   last   firsts   on   fire.
this   mountain   estranges.
this   is,   as   the   histories   call   it,   tore.
this   mine's   utter-ending   time
burned   in   its   mind   escapes   solder-told   story:
we   thought   ours   tightest,   might-made.   upend   it.
time   grown   out   of   and   away   to   as   one   tends,
like   this   note   is   aspen   trembling   there.

[TEST]

it's not that I don't work, it's that I can't hold a charge.
replace   meant   so   sighed   per   this   day:
his   isn't   to   be   her.   aim   over.
we,   the   last   one,   too   late.
ever only after is scar-struck, the last firs on fire,
his   mountain   ranges,
his   is   as   the   historical lit ore,
his   minute   rending   time,
burned   in   is   mindscape's older old   story:
we   thought   our   sight   might,   made-up,   end   it.
I'm   grown   out   of   and   away   to   a   one ends
like   this: no   is   a   pen   trembling   here.

WRIT IN FIRE

Burden,
burned.

DO[OR]

The dream redacted cannot sleep; it whimpers
so relentlessly of lost particulars . . .

—Amy Clampitt, "The Burning Child"

I.

do[   ]

sound reforms,
sour re-quiets around read roses
in orbits of it,

oracle argues sing

too, taled a recording scratched. i bled one

> more and one red or—too—risen, able.

   [or]

sun deforms,
sure, quiets a run. dead roses
in bits of it,

a clear guessing

totaled are coding scratch, edible. done

> mean done red to is enable.

II.

do[   ]

open nerve roars certains
so to asterisk now.

i onto or say
a so viral swept.
ichor a sea wore.

swore port off
of finish out rally out old me
as if on order,
solid strung—
we'll see nascent idea for more, lore, ore
into swore at—oh, avert!—asked ours
on, restless.

    [or]

pen never ascertains
so taste is know

into o say
as vials wept
i chase a we

swept off,
off in i shut all you told me
as i, fonder,
slid stung,
well seen, a scent i, deaf, melee
into sweat, have tasked us
nestless.

III.

do[   ]

bored of fortune,
inch as miles to destroyer—very—a spore never grown

next one starred
               a so-break-in
is not brought

over tone and so-a-liar slips
other of all art out so scarred—

a show as art
                owing rip art from
go in go wrestle avert uneasy out ease
loose nothing's trope, den smothers
and i mend all that

   [or]

bed off tune,
in chasm i lest odes try every aspen ever grown

next nest a red
                  as beak in
isn't bought

overt one and's alias lips
the fall at outs scared

ash was at
                wing i part from
going west leaver tune as you tease
loosen thing stop eden's mothers

and i'm—end all that

IV.

do[   ]

i'm no wounder.
  rest. i mated court with swore at (made more or less)
    soar i sketch in organ only air-   court, a sober goring one, a torn ever.

i omit run, dress in grays,   be star in sore, make so, forgive.

dis-ordain there actor orchard us there tore arid rooted one rid a so rift uneasy our
soons rear, soons raze a lot's voiced respite i dolor of flat choirs heave only draught
   erases pied

sound recycles around roses i story raging, i ordeal.
mouth full of arils forest i've over yes cape grown so wrings out humors

as chore me recourses

                open drips into

has typo rages on and on over serrating itself

       a skin so reamed

leave other more so strip so a priori torch far mother tongue of ire lord in of army
a so farther we stand a together ardor against oars is

no worst arbor right new messages, ours
before arrest less for, adored us.

true or false: loose draft.   the one who merits   owns to art. ring

around earth as what a catch can. done
blamed origin to a story ore so totaled, rocked

oar-calloused upriver, a ceded eon rowing, run redacted out of its history.

or so lord i error aport.

   [or]

i'm now under,
      estimated, cut with. sweat made me less
         so, a risk etching an only air.   cut as begin gone at never

i'm it undressing rays   best a rinse makes of give.

disdain the react char dust here tear i'd rote done i'd as if tune as your
son's reasons—a zealot's vice despite idol off latch is heavenly daughter as espied

sun decycles a run, doses is try aging ideal.
mouth full, fails. festive very escape gown swings out hums

a scheme recuses

      pen dips into

hasty pages on and no verse rating itself.

      ask in seamed

leave the mess, tip sap i itch farm the tongue field infamy
as far the west and at get heard again stasis

now star bright new mess ages us
be fear restless faded us.

true/false: lose daft   the new home its   own starting.

a run death as what a catch, can-done.
blame, dig in. toast yes to tale docked,

a call used up. i've raced eden owing, run red, acted outfits, his toy

soldier, rapt.

V.

do[   ]

see in. go threw it.
moon-eyed ranger's
priors tine a sound, error
of a dress and stored
now, rioter
ago, rain.

   [**or**]

seeing the wit
moneyed, anger's
pristine asunder
fades sands to red.
no. write
again.

As One within a Swoon –
Goes safely – where an open eye –
Would drop Him – Bone by Bone –

—Emily Dickinson, "There is a pain—
  so utter" (1863)

*

an acre hidden between eros *and its errors*

—Elizabeth Willis, "A Maiden"

SOMETHING WONDERFUL IS ABOUT TO HAPPEN TO YOU

Say Fortune's a poem without blood? Nope. Hung it.
Beauty flaws out, opens through omen. Pit no *I do*
against itself. Moon, why out too deep? Oh, burn up
our bodies. Flow. Punish. Too on path, augment, yet
let *or . . . but . . .* shape the map. Soon now, you unfit god, I
won't need to sough, to blue mouth, pray of. I spin a
poor pain if owed to one, sought asylum but then
what bout of pangs honed imperiously? Tune too,
too, too us. Adieu? Nothing but my flower happens.

WRIT IN MOTION

(Epitaph in
it: *I* happen.)

ROAD   NOT   END

no   dear   don't

read   into   it.   Instead
edits   read   an   *it*   into

as   in   *to*   *be*   meant   *to*   *bite*
bet   beast   ate   in   motion.

Redaction   is   a
red   action   is   a

scarlet
scar   let

shine.   Cycles
clinch   yeses

yes   inks   out   a   moan   now   *no*.
As   you   know   *no*   means   *into*.

TUNED : LIT

<pre>
gut   tug.
it's   split.   it's   spilt.
i un-gave   vague in

this   mistake.
this   time,   ask.

ask is   a kiss
into   other   words
drew   in   too   short

(rife: fire   ::   dire   :   ride)

as   a   skeleton
asks   not   alee

as   we   reckoned
wreck   a   need   so

in ghost   so night

so   be   it.   day   stabs
as   it   (a   body)   bests.

at   itself,   a   feather
flies   at   the   after,   a
</pre>

what : thaw :: my dear : my dare

begins.   sing.   be.

born,   so   cries,   sir.   bled
on   scribbled   sorries.

i drew : we rid :: into : not i

hey, no : honey :: these eyes : see the yes

i   was   angry   at
try   again,   saw

the   myth   as
maths   they

(i)   minus.
in   us   i'm

add-led,   addled

to   the   slaughter.
utter   *heal,*   *ghost.*

a   scar   is   a   ghost   and   vice
versa,   a   sad   so   catching   i

threw   up   my   hand.   so
shape   why   not   drum

material   a trial me

haunts   as hunt

43

undead   and due

indeed   i'd need

hot wax   what *xo*

kiss   oft   in   an   ether   or

i   ask   in   nether-soft   or

then your italics *if/then* wove pull for fine delight
i voted for the first punch line: *you will feel a thing.*

we   all   felt   it   and   it   won.
welted   twin,   flail   no   at

strip   this   trips   this

ask   is   a   kiss

is   ask   a   kiss

is   ask   a   kiss.

[COS(IGN]EOUS)

So lines crag us away, slide phantom. I'm log-
outed, passworn again. Yes, I chasm. I'll glom
onto a missing edge, lay as law, slum orphic,
cop mysteries—*mah gawd*—in glossolalia, un-
ashored, tsunami's willing cog. Employ—as a
stylus gone seismographomaniacal wild—
my menial ghost, sacred slip on us ago, wail
a map is home, cue a song, try glissando, will
call whose slap rings out, sign *may I*, ado me
classy as a gold prom night limousine. *Awe*,
earth—glum god—yawns, soils as I open claim,
a meter maid I'll pay so, so, slow—changing us.

I DO

after Meg Ronan

Never meant, never meat, never met.
Try a break. Buckle up. Weary query
gut put after all. A last jab, haze, hex.

Beneath the mattress, guns. Stutter.
Stumble, crazy easy. Keep just a fuck,
bequeath the rest. Laws vex, amaze—

all next level parlay. Bet a jester's last
laugh. Full cuff freeze, luck up a sleeve,
squats, lunges. But we came bulletless.

CRY UNTO   COUNTRY

Mind as conflagration,
mind as a canting floor—

not as in
nation's

raw red
reward—

rather some
other mare's

lore—plays up a
role. Apply us a

poultice of pulped bills
(cut, I bleed). Poll's pupil, of

this sea be fealty's fashion. I
obey, finish a last shift, see a

say-sickness, to swab
abscess, ways to skin

late cataplasm,
a meat past call.

Spend us
sends up

baubles, sad
baud, bless a

bit per second,
bent crop dies,

honored
horde. On

a bruising
in us I brag
as big ruin—

In America
I can re-aim.

THIS, CERTAIN

Ich streue das weisse Nichts . . .

—Unica Zürn

I scatter the white nothing.
Tonight cites thin weather.
I trace twine to thighs, then
wrist, then tighten. I echo at
teeth, chatter this: *I, no wing.*

Q & A

But haven't others done all this before?

To belief, heaven's both holster and rut.

[innovation's
invasion, not

mid-progress as
promised, grass

greener and heart at
earth, a tender range]

Is it just a word game?

Is a god just wartime?

THEN READING   IN THE GARDEN

my iris, know	i risk my now
for you.	for you,
fuchsia, intent.	if us, then i can't
stand coping,	stop dancing.
all this stupid heat,	a stall, the *up* *this* i'd
tend to	dent. to
what's left: it's this last weft,	the last swift,
stitches in	its chest. in
thrust, be a sure	suture. breaths
stake my	sky, meat
left looser,	lost reel of
pure monster, no petal	nor stem. rope un-leapt
dares *show*,	re-shadows.
i drown in the wind or in the	when. i, rind to
sweet segments, us,	wet guess, net mess,
loss.	loss
is spent	in steps,
into	it no
answer.	re-swan,
answer	as wren,
bird called	bed rid, call

outs	and	inners,
and	i	grit,
a	line,
veered	into.

no, i wound. i didn't hit a wall
spot	on.	in	pleasing	us,
no	night's	fortune
spent,	no
not	memory,
we	love	a
but we vow aweather, and in-
can find me sore,	end from *in case*.
a	swear:
the last poor excuses for
sea, a word is my bond, but
it	fate,	then	and	now?
up?	sad	old	itch?	still.

sand	in	our	nest
daring	it.
lane	i
need	it	over.

i hit a window, all not undid,
a	song	split	us	open.	in
tunes	for	nothing
not	pens,
not	my	*more.*
vow	alee
bound. i want whatever awe
if rose can mend
was,	*are,*
force : aster, phlox, suet, so
my bonds are outbid. was
a	theft	i	went	on	and
all	this	stupid	cold.

See through me. See me through.

For partings hurt although we dip the pain
Into a glowing well—the pen I mean.
Living alone won't make some inmost face to shine
Maned with light, ember and anodyne,
Deep in a desktop burnished to its grain.
That the last hour be learned again
By riper selves, couldn't you doff this green
Incorruptible, the might-have-been,

And arm in arm with me dare the magician's tent?
It's hung with asterisks.

—James Merrill, "Yánnina"

AFTER PLATH: METAPHORS I

[*I'm a riddle in nine syllables,*]

Stealing a safe view, interstate
still a smooth read, nothing in
mirrors, not need or glint, not even
a least glimmer in the rims of a coupe
so far. An on-ramp's best offer is belief,
yes, spell an easy does it and I bite,
finally sing assent, an infinity.
Big rig, add a deep rumble now,
the true coup down the highway.

AFTER PLATH: METAPHORS II

[An elephant, a ponderous house,]

Not to faint at blood, a creeping
up in the syringe, I avert my eyes then
run, or else. I'll feint so at a mind's
view, my unlit corners. My wild
ape meat is a treif menu in a red pen.
I'd eat. I see a starting pistol's first
green shoot, a bean's beginning in
a fêted barrel, a flash and slosh,
swim of a goldfish bowl on the go.

AFTER PLATH: METAPHORS III

[*A melon strolling on two tendrils.*]

Call me Big Ag, I brag,
tending the feedlot and warehouse,
silo and hormones, pen, seed, rib.
From newly iffy memory, I recite
whose maple syrup taps these are
and so on. Inning's stint as dafter sieve,
inning as moist ort. All in a different vein,
I say, tiring, out of breath, panting
as the balloon I tie taut swells.

AFTER PLATH: METAPHORS IV

[O red fruit, ivory, fine timbers!]

Aviary, apiary, one warm swarm
and flutter. Bubble tea, puff pastry,
lit fuse, ore. I reel, dine asea.
Greeting-card sentiments, honey
dripping into the moss-lined nest
of a loon, wings riled in the offing.
Motor revs, then idles. A magician's
assistant, smiling to be sawed in half,
saying I'll be the one, the one too.

AFTER PLATH: METAPHORS V

[*This loaf's big with its yeasty rising.*]

A nature documentary. Opening
shot, pan, a narrator's measured
tone intent on saying stab, storm,
life, flap, ash, bone, tool, till, life,
death. So yes, as I listen, I begin
to believe I'm the whole sorry
shebang, finding my mess the stained
sign of an entire paradigm. I, inverted
flower we call fruit, fig wasp inside.

AFTER PLATH: METAPHORS VI

[Money's new-minted in this fat purse.]

I've been a flag left planted on
a distant planet, its sea singing
in an empty shell, a file sighing
stone to sand. See if I defy eye,
defy firmament. Petri's eager agar,
proverbial whore to culture, embrace
what blooms in a windowless room
in a laboratory rinsed in sun's hot
tints shining from the inside out.

AFTER PLATH: METAPHORS VII

[*I'm a means, a stage, a cow in calf.*]

Mob's all thumbs in the Colosseum,
meat thrown to a dull roar as gears
engage, meat in a trendy blender.
A spy in internal affairs, other shoe
dropping, in me, it's pints of rennet
in a stein, gift pony, baloney sandwich
with a side of live wires, eel's vitals,
fine dust, fine lines—fine. I'm
a gag order to go. Bye. Ate it.

AFTER PLATH: METAPHORS VIII

[I've eaten a bag of green apples,]

I'm a full load of delicates, spin de siècle.
I weight my turn as if willing paint to dry—
yes, no, maybe, no, not even—as if
pushing at aspen apron strings
to resist a nesting doll's tight fit.
In a drawer between bones
free of name, see a Sunday roast,
high tide, barge, loom, harvest moon,
entire fire ant hill in amber.

AFTER PLATH: METAPHORS IX

[Boarded the train there's no getting off.]

I'm loop-the-loop, cat that swallowed
the caboose, wild oat-stuffed feed bag,
my mailman's worst nightmare. Holes in
a belt let out—dormant nine-eyed
serpent. I, darling hive, as-is
abyss, open infight, inner
tuber's inner fryer. Pain, again.
Endless Tetris turning on my if, if, if.
A siege-long season arrives. I ante.

Notes

Essay   **as yes,**—The third stanza borrows phrasing and thinking from Samuel Kinser's "Saussure's Anagrams: Ideological Work" (*MLN* 94, no. 5, 1979). "Sous rature" (under erasure) is a philosophical device conceived of by Martin Heidegger. "[Unica] Zürn's 'old, dangerous fever'" refers to her description of her own anagrammatic poetics as "the old, dangerous fever of the anagrams." "[Nathaniel] Mackey's 'exegetic sweat'" borrows from "Ghost of a Trance," in which he writes, "We / were chill, shiver, exegetic sweat, backed- / up interpreters put upon by sluff, none / of us could say what was what." "Love me little, love me long, / is the burden of my song" is the refrain of an anonymous sixteenth-century poem.

Stet—*Merriam-Webster* defines the verb "stet" as "to direct retention of (a word or passage previously ordered to be deleted or omitted from a manuscript or printer's proof) by annotating usually with the word *stet*." The word is of Latin origin, from *stare*, "to stand"; *stet* translates roughly as "let it stand." Formally, this poem proceeds through anagramming, as is the case with the majority of the poems in this book (though the use of redaction is also a recurring formal choice). In this poem, every line is an anagram of every other line. Other poems use the anagram slightly differently, for example, by anagramming fragments within individual lines or proceeding couplet by couplet anagrammatically.

face to Hex—This poem is an erasure of "Postface to Hexentexte" by Hans Bellmer, translated by Pierre Joris, from *Hexentexte* by Unica Zürn.

lay and   **try**—This poem is an erasure of "Play and Poetry," by Johan Huizinga, from *Homo Ludens* (English translation, Roy Publishers, 1950).

Writ in Ore—This title, along with those of "Writ in Fire" and "Writ in Motion," alludes to John Keats's epitaph, "Here lies One Whose Name was writ in Water."

Something wonderful is about to happen to you—This title was found in a fortune cookie.

tuned : lit—The phrase "You will feel a thing" was the winner of the *New Yorker*'s March 31, 2014 Cartoon Caption Contest, submitted by Brent McCafferty of Great Falls, Montana.

I do—This poem owes a debt to Meg Ronan's "Epithalamion for Out-laws: Ace Hiporst (for Sara Nicholson and C. Violet Eaton)" (*The The*, 2014). Ronan's poem is a version of the "beautiful outlaw (*belle absente*)," described by the *Oulipo Compendium* as follows:

> *The outlaw in question is the name of the person (or subject) to whom the poem is addressed. Each line of the poem includes all the letters of the al-phabet except for the letter appearing in the dedicated name at the position corresponding to that of the line . . . The beautiful outlaw, which belongs to the category of lipograms, recreates the traditional acrostic as an absence instead of the presence of a name.*

"I do" takes liberties with the form, in that all three title letters are absent from the entire poem, and the alphabet repeats by stanza, not line. The-matically, Ronan's epithalamion endured, if darkly.

Cry unto   Country—The phrase "Cut, I bleed" alludes to Shylock's "If you prick us, do we not bleed?" from Shakespeare's *The Merchant of Venice*.

This, Certain—The epigraph "*Ich streue das weisse Nichts*" translates to the poem's first line, "I scatter the white nothing." The line is from Unica Zürn's 1954 *Hexentexte* ("Witches' Text" or "Witches' Writings"), her col-lection of anagram poems.

Q & A—The final line obliquely references the aphorism "There are no atheists in foxholes," the origin of which is uncertain.

After Plath: Metaphors I–IX—Each poem in this series is an anagram of the entirety of Sylvia Plath's poem "Metaphors." The nine lines of Plath's poem, in chronological order, also serve as epigraphs for each

poem in the series. The final lines of "After Plath: Metaphors V" owe a
debt to Jessica Hudgins's poem "On the Failure of Mutually Beneficial
Relationships" (*The Journal* 40, no. 1, 2016).